Pump it up Magazine

TABLE OF CONTENTS

⚡ **EDITORIAL** 6
Page 5

⚡ **REVIEW** 11
How Music For Roller Rink Impacted The Club

⚡ **STYLE** 21
70's Fashion is Back!

⚡ **MUST WATCH** 28
Best Rollerskaking Movies of All Time!

⚡ **FREDA PAYNE**
Legendary Song Stylist FREDA PAYNE Returns w/ Star-Studded Jazz Duets EP Let There Be Love

⚡ **WHAT'S HOT!**
- Mother's Day: Unique Songs about Moms
- Get Ready To Go Out L.A. Best Spot!
- Modern Recording Artist Hand Book By Bernie Capodici

⚡ **BEAUTY**
Spring Time Detox

⚡ **TOP TIPS**
Creative Ways To Sell More Merch

⚡ **HUMANITARIAN AWARENESS**
Together We Can End Hunger

Pump it up
MAGAZINE

PUMP IT UP MAGAZINE
LINKS

WEBSITE
www.pumpitupmagazine.com

FACEBOOK
www.facebook.com/pumpitupmagazine

TWITTER
www.twitter.com/pumpitupmag

SOUNDCLOUD
www.soundcloud.com/pumpitupmagazine

INSTAGRAM
pumpitupmagazine

PINTEREST
www.pinterest.com/pumpitupmagazine

PUMP IT UP MAGAZINE
30721 Russell Ranch Road
Suite 140
Westlake Village,
California 91362
United States
www.pumpitupmagazine.com
info@pumpitupmagazine.com
Tel : (001) (877)841 – 7414 (toll free number)

EDITORIAL

Greetings Readers,

Is Spring really here? Wow! how time flies when we are partially locked down in this Covid era. But there is light at the end of the tunnel so hang in there and observe the logic of events unfold hopefully in a positive way for all.

On the cover, rising R&B icon Saint Jaimz launches back onto the global music scene with his latest unforgettable EP "Throw Back the Covers (Vol. 1).
The six-track epic is a compilation of the most timeless R&B tracks to grace us over the past few decades. "Throwback, The Covers" (Vol.1) is moving up the charts.

We have new music by amazing indie artists, and EM (our November 2020 cover girl) 's single Say What You Mean is now on Billboard charts among mainstream royalties!

Last but not least, I am happy to announce the release of my first Smooth Jazz album in America. It's called "Satisfied" I hope you will like it. You may pre-order CD and or Vinyl on my website www.Aneessa.com

Musicians and Artists, be sure to read about NFT's. It's overtaking the Music Industry

As usual, we have our Beauty section with Anti-aging secrets.

Our Fashion section is all about the '90s.

There are more Music industry tips and music documentaries to check out and in our humanitarian awareness section we bring your attention to the sensitive and caring subject of Autism with a focus on World Autism Awareness Day, April 2, 2021

So, flip through the pages of this edition and, don't forget to tune in to Pump It Up Magazine Radio where all the hits are played, and listen to our independent Spotify Playlist who has gathered more than 13k followers!

Be safe and be blessed!!

Anissa Boudjaoui

CONTRIBUTORS

EDITOR IN CHIEF
Anissa Boudjaoui

MUSIC
Michael B. Sutton
A. Scott Galloway
Sarah Kaye

FASHION
Tiffani Sutton

MARKETING
Grace Rose

PARTNERS

Editions L.A.
www.editions-la.com

The Sound Of L.A.
www.thesoundofla.com

Info Music
www.infomusic.fr

Delit Face
www.DelitFace.com

L.A. Unlimited
www.launlimitedinc.com

Legendary Song Stylist FREDA PAYNE Returns w/ Star-Studded Jazz Duets EP Let There Be Love –

Triple-Threat vocal wonder Freda Payne returns from a 6-year sabbatical with her most star-studded Jazz vocal project yet, Let There Be Love. The 5-song EP - in the tradition of 10-inch shellac records from the golden years of jazz – is bubbling over with knockout performances highlighted by 4 duets with special guests who are not only stellar singers, they ALL exude sparkling chemistry with Ms. Payne. Recorded inside fabled Capitol Records Studio 'A' in Hollywood and officially releasing via The Sound of L.A. Records on Friday April 16, this instant classic from Freda and company will surely be one of the finest Jazz Vocal projects of 2021.

With big band charts for 30-pieces by Grammy-winner Gordon Goodwin and production by Rodrigo Rios (Executive Produced by Michael Goetz for Alain Franke Music), no expense was spared to make Ms. Payne's return a spectacular one. The first single (released in November) is a dream come true duet with Johnny Mathis on the George & Ira Gershwin gem "They Can't Take That Away From Me," filled with sweetly flirtatious energy and the spirit of the singular Nelson Riddle. 2021 Grammy-winner for Best Jazz Vocal Album, Kurt Elling, swings in to join Freda on a rhapsodic scat symphony of Gershwin's "Our Love is Here to Stay." Freda has a field day with Michigan friend Dee Dee Bridgewater on the ingenious medley "Moanin' n' Doodlin'" which pairs up two lyricized jazz gems from the pens of piano greats Bobby Timmons ("Moanin'") and Horace Silver ("Doodlin'"). Soul crooner Kenny Lattimore slides in next to Freda for a cool jazz meets mod-pop reading of the ol' Nat King Cole hit, "Let There Be Love." Finally, Ms. Payne trades scats solo with the band on the sassy "It's Alright With Me," delivering fans shades of Ella that served her well across the decades.

Though internationally renowned for her chart-topping 1970 Soul-Pop classic "Band of Gold," Ms. Payne began her career in 1962 singing Jazz. She has since lent voice to everything from standards, R&B and Quiet Storm to Disco and Pop.

The last two decades have found Freda Payne firmly back home in Jazz.

Her latest, Let There Be Love, will make lovers of the genre giddy - from vets to newbies

FREDA PAYNE

"I wanted a hit so bad to boost my career. Now that I've got this hit, people think I'm a soul singer and I'm not. And I have to sing it everywhere. And I had to sing songs that were similar. Jazz was my thing."

Freda Payne

REVIVING THE ICONIC SOUND OF JAZZ MUSIC

www.FredaPayne.com

FREDA PAYNE

WHAT FIRST GOT YOU INTO MUSIC?

Taking piano lessons and studying the American song book.

WHO INSPIRED YOU TO MAKE MUSIC?

Ella Fitzgerald and Gloria Lynn

HOW WERE YOU ABLE TO GET THESE GREAT ARTISTS TO PERFORM ON YOUR NEW ALBUM?

My producer Rodrigo Rios contacted the manager of each artist. I got Kenny Lattimore my self.

DID YOU ENJOY WORKING WITH ONE ARTIST MORE THAN ANOTHER ON THIS ALBUM?

NO.. I enjoyed each artist just as much as the other.

HOW DO YOU FEEL THE INTERNET HAS IMPACTED THE MUSIC BUSINESS?

It has dealt a devastating blow to the bottom line of the record business financially.

WHICH FAMOUS MUSICIANS DO YOU ADMIRE?

Miles Davis, Sting, Stevie Wonder, Herbie Hancock, Duke Ellington, George Benson, Horace Silver, John Legend, Kenny G. Santana, Herbert & Ronnie Laws, Chick Corea

WHAT IS THE BEST ADVICE YOU'VE BEEN GIVEN?

Is to begin right is to end right!!

WHAT'S NEXT FROM YOU?

I have some shows scheduled in the U.K. in September. Will be doing some talk show, Pe Palm Springs in November 10, 2021 at the McCallum Theatre a show called One Night Only. My book will be released in the fall.

EDITIONS L.A.

GRAPHIC AND WEB **DESIGN**

WEBSITE
CD COVER
LOGO
FLYER
BANNERS
EPK
LYRICS VIDEO
TRANSLATION

We give you the tools to make your song or band to be heard around the world !

**INFO@
EDITIONS-L.A.COM**

WWW.EDITIONS-LA.COM

SPECIAL **OFFERS** 50% ON LYRICS VIDEOS
HIGH-QUALITY MUSIC LYRICS VIDEO
UP TO 1080P HD VIDEO QUALITY
MODERN AND SIMPLE STYLE
$250 FOR MUSIC VIDEO UP TO 4 MIN
$350 FOR MUSIC VIDEO UP TO 5 MIN

FOR MORE INFO VISIT WWW.EDITIONS-LA.COM

HOW MUSIC FOR THE ROLLER RINK IMPACTED THE CLUB

Moodymann's Soul Skate party embodies a long tradition where rollerskating and club music intertwine. We spoke with Kenny Dixon Jr., Traci Washington, Louie Vega, Danny Krivit and more on one of America's richest subcultures.

When you show up to Detroit's Northland Roller Rink during Soul Skate, you enter a different world. Thousands of skaters, along with a few hundred Moodymann fans, crowd onto the burnished hardwood floor. Look closely, and you'll observe nuanced regional skate styles honed in cities like Atlanta, Philadelphia and LA throughout the year. Skate scene DJs like DJ Arson play sub-110 BPM grooves to keep things rolling smooth. Detroit locals greet visitors like family. 80-year-olds put you to shame on skates.

Back in 2007, I showed up at Northland for the first Soul Skate. A free soul food buffet was on offer. Around 3 AM, the rink cleared out for "roll call," in which skaters showed off different regional styles—JB (James Brown-style skating) from Chicago, fast backwards from Philly/Jersey, Detroit's slide-heavy "open house" variant—while onlookers lined the rails. The event felt convivial, wholesome, about as far from the hedonistic Movement afterparty scene as you could get.

A decade and change later, Soul Skate is on the map as a national skate jam. 2018's edition was basically a small festival, with three rinks and a four-day programme that included things like an indoor picnic, a documentary screening and an adult prom.

"That was truly a mistake," said Kenny Dixon Jr., AKA Moodymann, on Soul Skate's escalation from local party to national festival. I spoke with him in the iconic, purple-curtained house he owns on Grand Boulevard, just across the street from Submerge, a noted local record store and headquarters for Underground Resistance. "Really it started out as, 'How can I put everybody in one room and focus on them buying my T-shirts?'" he said. "I wanna put everybody in there and smother them with my record label, my artists, my T-shirts. That was one of the ideas for Soul Skate, and then that flopped and people didn't give a fuck about my T-shirts or my product or my records. They were like, 'When's your next skate party?'" He laughed. "Yeah, it's its own monster now."

Since the mid-20th century, skating rinks have been an extraordinary staging ground for music and DJ culture, to say nothing of their importance within the civil rights movement and as a gathering space for black communities. As real estate in American cities becomes more scarce and rinks in black neighborhoods disappear, national skate jams like Soul Skate have become a crucial environment for a scene steeped in a tradition that continues to flourish.

Louie Vega, who fell in love with music and DJing as a teenage skater during New York City's early '80s skate boom, returned to the rink to DJ Soul Skate in 2014. "It's beautiful that Moodymann and the Soul Skate team stick to the roots and show where it comes from," he said over the phone. "Skating music has a lot to do with R&B and dance, just as much as discos and house clubs."

Style skating—a skate-dancing style that has splintered into hundreds of regional variants—got its start, in a roundabout way, in Detroit. Bill Butler started skating in 1945 at the Arcadia Ballroom on Woodward Avenue in Detroit on the one night black people were allowed in. At the time, skating rinks were typically scored by chintzy organ music, but on black nights they played records like Count Basie's "Night Train," Ella Fitzgerald's "Do Nothin' Till You Hear From Me" and Duke Ellington's "C Jam Blues." Years later, as an air force sergeant stationed in Alaska, Butler won money for a pair of skates in a game of craps and started developing his signature "jamma" style, his movements mirroring the solos on the jazz records he'd skate to. He was assigned to an air force station in Brooklyn in 1957 and showed up at the nearest rink, Empire Rollerdrome, where mostly black skaters were rolling to live organ music. He approached the woman in charge and asked if she would play "Night Train." The needle dropped and style skating changed forever.

Legendary skate DJ and Soul Skate regular Big Bob Clayton refers to the now-closed Empire Rollerdrome as the "the birthplace of roller disco." Clayton, a New York native, has been DJing for 50 years.

"Most of the dance skating today, you see them holding hands and doing their moves, that's jam skating, that's Bill. That's Bill Butler all day," Clayton said. "I used to go to Empire in '69, but I wasn't worried about DJing in the skate world, I went there because I liked the hustle. I'd go there and dance, I'd skate for the first two hours, then the next two hours, I would hustle in the middle. We were all skaters and dancers, so a friend came to me once in '77 and say, 'Yo Bob, you ever think about DJing in the skate world?' I said, 'Nah man, I'm a club head, I like the club scene.'" He rattled off a list of legendary NYC haunts. "The Loft, Better Days, that's where I liked to be at... I've been playing club music and house music ever since the '70s. That's what I came from."

Clayton started DJing for skaters in '77, eventually landing enviable rink residencies at The Roxy, then at the mecca itself, Empire, both of which were outfitted with soundsystems designed by Richard Long, the legendary audio architect who built the systems at Paradise Garage and Studio 54 in New York and Warehouse in Chicago, to name just a few. Clayton began immersing himself in regional music and skate styles. The folk music anthologist Harry Smith used to have a party trick where he'd identify the county a singer was born in from one verse of a song. Clayton is the skate world equivalent.

"Every state and city had their own style," he said. Locking arms and traversing the rink in trains came from Detroit, for instance. "The hitch-kicking in the line came from Detroit. When you do a bow-legged move like this on your skates"—Clayton spreads his knees in his chair as though he's on skates—"it's called a grapevine. Came out of Detroit. If you want to see all the fast backwards stuff, that came out of South Jersey and Philly, and the Delaware area. I could talk to you about this for hours."

Beginning in the mid-'80s, Clayton traveled to rinks around the US. "I heard about wherever the adults were skating in each city and I would just go. They knew me from Florida to Buffalo, but a lot of cities didn't know who I was when I showed up. I would just pay my money, come in and stand around and I say, 'Oh, they play this here, or they skate like this to that music.' I took notes, I wrote stuff down. Bill gave me the incentive to do that. He traveled all over the country and brought this jamma technique. And that's how I got into the game. So for almost two decades, there was nobody out there but me, because nobody else knew what to do."

As Clayton made strides as a national skate DJ, he remained part of a coterie of NYC DJs and musicians that included Larry Levan, Nicky Siano and Boyd Jarvis. "Even though I was a skate DJ, they knew I loved club and house music, but I made my money in the skate world. Levan was the man. I'd leave Empire at four, five in the morning and go to the Garage. We learned from each other and I brought it to the skate world. When I first started taking out the bass and the highs, all the other DJs around the country at the rinks were like, 'What the hell does he keep doing to the music?'"

Clayton played the adult prom at last year's Soul Skate, holding court in front of a room of skaters who had switched out their wheels for heels and patent leather shoes. He attends every Soul Skate and regularly advises the team of 14 who run the event, which includes Rafael Bryant (Smooth Skatin Ralph), Demarco Bearden (Gadget), Joann Johnson (JoJo), Marcus Gavin (Fresh) and Maurice Dortch (Moe).

"Me and Kenny [Dixon Jr.], we met in the early '90s," Clayton said. "He was skating and hanging out then. This was before he had the record label... Kenny is a beautiful brother. He treats me like a god. He picked me up in a Suburban looking like I'm the president, being whisked through the city. They take good care of me and the respect is there."

The Soul Skate hospitality isn't only afforded to skate legends like Clayton. When I told Dixon Jr. I'd attended various Soul Skate events in 2018, he asked with genuine concern if I'd had a good time and apologized for how hot it had been. "It was way too many people last time," he said. "Apologies for that.

Speaking with Dixon Jr., who has agreed to only two interviews over the last decade, was never a sure thing. We were originally meant to meet up at Detroit Roller Wheels for a morning skate session he frequents, but he was due at DGTL Festival in Amsterdam the next day, and I was informed last-minute he wouldn't be able to make it. Undeterred, I drove out to the rink, a colourful building on an otherwise drab stretch of Schoolcraft St., on a cloudy Friday morning. Inside, a DJ played slow R&B jams like "Get To Know Ya" by Maxwell and "Insanity" by Gregory Porter. Regulars greeted each other with hugs on the side of the rink. A regal older couple glided by with one leg up in perfectly synced figure-skating style.

Traci Washington, Dixon Jr.'s right-hand, turned up a little before noon. After greeting a few skaters, we settled into a booth at the snack bar. I asked her how she got into skating.

"My daughter is now 21, but when she was in middle school, probably 13, they'd have skating trips," she said. "Often times during the day the rinks are reserved for school parties, so I went as a chaperone. I told Kenny about the party and he came over and once I saw what his body was doing on skates I was like, 'What in the world is going on here? What is that?' He was skating around children, jumping over kids that fell, simultaneously helping kids up, adeptly cutting through crowds of children. It just made me want to acquire that level—if not that level of skill—just to use my body as a form of art."

She went on: "No matter how tired he is he'll get off a flight from overseas and get to the rink that night. And he'll find skating sessions. If he's in London he'll find a place to skate. So it's a private way for him to enjoy himself. He is extremely humble, he doesn't promote himself or Mahogani Music." She gestured toward the rink. "These people in here don't know anything about Moodymann. They'll just say, 'Hey Kenny, how you doin'?' And he's always happy to see them and they're happy to see him."

At the rink, the swagger of Moodymann's persona slips away. It occurred to me that he's not interested in interviews because he's not interested in self-promotion. He's concerned with giving back to the community, whether it's throwing a BBQ in his backyard or handing out copies of his latest, unreleased LP. After I left Detroit Roller Wheels, I spoke to him on the phone. We talked about Soul Skate, Big Bob Clayton and that morning's skate session. He told me to come over to his house in an hour. Knocking on the door of his house on Grand, purple curtains blowing in the wind, felt like finally meeting a mythical, Wizard Of Oz-like character.

"That party is for Detroit," Dixon Jr. said. "We take an L every time, it takes us two years to recoup, save up and get money. But we're in the negative every year."

Due to the wave of rink closures, Dixon Jr. explained, skating has become a road trip culture. "For example, a lot of us skaters travel. But there are a lot of skaters that hear about the out-of-town parties and they can't travel. They don't have the means or the funds. We decided, why don't we just bring it to them? A lot of people ask me, how come you're not DJing or the regular rink DJ is not there? It's because, in a lot of ways, that's the same stuff we hear on a weekly basis. The idea of this here is bringing out-of-town people to Soul Skate is so, one, they can enjoy all the out-of-towners they don't usually get the opportunity to see, and two, so we can show them Detroit hospitality and make sure everyone's having a good time."

At each Soul Skate there's an unannounced headliner at Northland on Saturday night. In 2016, Dixon Jr., dressed immaculately in a white suit and straw campaign hat, introduced hip-hop legend Rakim. In 2018, a curtain dropped, revealing soul music legend Ronald Isley to a screaming, adoring audience gathered on the wood floor of the rink.

I asked Dixon Jr. if the Detroit skaters know he's a house music institution, jetting off to play festivals every weekend. "A few," he said. "It leaks out because you got the internet now. But have I officially come out and agreed to any of that shit? No," he laughed. "Going over there is providing a way for me to do things like this. To give people a concert they didn't even know was coming to them. They might have not seen Rakim. Or, you know, believe it or not, you got people that skate and will skip out on dinner or provide for their children, and I got a full course meal, you know? Try to keep it all night. I got food. Don't leave talkin' about you're hungry, I gotta go and I'm hungry. I got that for you. Don't leave cause you gotta go to a club to see some other thing. I got a concert for you. You ain't gotta go nowhere, it's all tonight baby. Plenty of motherfuckers from all around on the floor."

Back at Detroit Roller Wheels, Washington told me how the national skate community found out about Detroit and Soul Skate. "The largest party in the country was started by a woman from Detroit called Joi," she said. "It's this huge party called Sk8-A-Thon, held during labor day weekend in Atlanta. At these parties, sometimes they'd give the flyers back, they'd say, 'Detroit? No, we're not coming up there.' Because we're known to be aggressive. I mean, we have a very smooth style of skating, but you go to Royal Skateland, these people like to slide, they're very protective of their territory and if you can't skate that style, you might get injured. I would meet hundreds, I would dare say thousands of people who skate and eventually, they got interested in coming here and the word spread."

She continued: "We're one of the few parties that's truly diverse. That's because we're serving house, techno, Moodymann fans and the black skate community throughout the country. Some of the parties around America, they're so big, you can't rent skates, you have to have your own, because they don't want anyone to get injured. We make sure at Soul Skate you can rent skates, because a lot of the people who made this party possible are fans of Moodymann."

Soul Skate is unique in that Dixon Jr., known for producing and DJing club music, is now a recognizable figure within the black skate community. They recognize his afro and sunglasses from Soul Skate T-shirts, not the cover of Silentintroduction. But skating culture is about music as much as it's about style skating and community.

"A good skate DJ plays like your parents at home,'" Dixon Jr. said. "They play like back in the '70s when you went to a club and they played everything. See, I can go to a club, get down, sweat, 'Boy, that shit was exciting,' me and my friends we would get down. We would have a great time, talk to the ladies… At the skate rink, they gonna slow it down, they gonna break it down, they gonna break it all the way down. You ain't gonna hear no slow jams at the club no more. Back in the '70s and '80s they'd rock you for about two hours and they'll break it back down."

Dixon Jr.'s sprawling Prince collection was neatly displayed on the walls around us at his Grand Blvd. house. "You're telling me you're not gonna play no 'Do Me Baby' in this bitch? The fuck? Fuck that."

The style of DJing Dixon Jr. is referring to has its roots in New York City's post-disco scene, when the loose, slowed-down sound developing on singles from classic Big Apple labels like Prelude worked just as well, or better, at the rink as they did in the club. The development of skate music from the late '70s up to the present is intertwined with the roots of dance music, as nuanced and colourful as any sub-genre.

THE SHIRELLES, "MAMA SAID"

Soul girl group The Shirelles made this grateful doo-wop bop, all about realizing mama knows best when it comes to heartbreak and love.

SAINT JAIMZ FEATY. KALEO ROSS , "HEY MA"

Only these guys could spin such a tender-hearted ballad for their moms. A great tribute to all the mothers in the world!

EMINEM, "CLEANIN' OUT MY CLOSET"

"I'm sorry momma / I never meant to hurt you." Never thought I'd relate to Eminem, but there's a first time for everything. Here's a rather earnest apology to Mama-nem, set to an infectiously smooth rat-a-tat rhythm.

BOYZ II MEN, "A SONG FOR MAMA"

Only these guys could spin such a tender-hearted ballad for their moms. If you really want to go all out, learn the piano part and give her a good old serenade.

TUPAC, "DEAR MAMA"

"I finally understand / For a woman it ain't easy trying to raise a man." 2pac's mom sounds like the absolute best, tbh.

B.B. KING, "NOBODY LOVES ME BUT MY MOTHER"

The King of the Blues knows what it's all about. Honestly, sometimes it really does feel that way.

SPICE GIRLS, "MAMA"

Just five gals sitting around on stools and singing about their moms. Thank you, 1996.

DELIT FACE

Social Media For The Entertainment World
MUSIC & MOVIE Industry

SINGER
SONGWRITER
MUSICIANS
PRODUCERS
PUBLISHERS
DISTRIBUTORS
MUSIC SUPERVISORS

ACTORS
DIRECTORS
PRODUCERS
DISTRIBUTORS
SET DESIGNERS
SCRIPT
WRITERS
EXTRAS

MAKE UP ARTISTS
HAIR STYLISTS
PHOTOGRAPHERS
GRAPHIC DESIGNER

Register now FREE and connect with people in your industry
www.delitface.com

WHAT'S HOT!

GET READY TO GO OUT! L.A. BEST SPOTS!

STROLL THROUGH THE STUNNING GARDENS AT THE HUNTINGTON LIBRARY

What is it? A historic library, museum and sprawling gardens that was the bequest of entrepreneur Henry E. Huntington.

Why go? The Huntington's distinctly themed gardens are easily the most stunning manicured outdoor spaces in SoCal. The library and museum are equally impressive, and reopen in mid-April; all require reservations.

Don't miss: Go for a stroll around the Chinese garden, which opened its massive expansion last fall. And make sure to see "Made in L.A.," which the Huntington is co-presenting with the Hammer Museum.

TRAVEL BACK IN TIME AT THE DRIVE-IN

What is it? About a half-dozen drive-in movie theaters in SoCal that are still going strong.

Why go? As theaters slowly reopen, it's one of the only ways to see a first-run movie right now that's not on your couch. But it's also tons of fun, cost effective and one of the few ways you can go out safely right now.

Don't miss: We particularly love the programming at Mission Tiki in Montclair. And look out for the occassional free screening or premieres thanks to familiar outlets like the ArcLight.

HAVE AN OCEANFRONT, ROADSIDE MEAL AT NEPTUNE'S NET

What is it? A postcard-worthy seafood shack on the Pacific Coast Highway toward the western edge of Malibu.

Why go? The fried ocean bites and weekend biker crew make Neptune's Net a unique destination. (Alternatively, dine up the coast with locals at Malibu Seafood, where the long line is worth the wait for fresh fish and seafood).

Don't miss: The famous spot is currently open with limited outdoor seating. So take your food across the street and park in the dirt patch by the water, with views of surfers and kite boarders.

YOUR MUSIC CONSULTANT

"YOU BELIEVE, SO DO WE!"

We Can Help You
To Grow Your Business

We are a monthly based service, we put faith in artists who has major potential, believed in them, and who are willing to spend their time and own money to work with us in building a successful music career!

Why
Choose Us ?

3 DECADES OF MUSIC BUSINESS EXPERIENCE
Platinum and Gold Records
MOTOWN RECORDS
UNIVERSAL
SONY
CAPITOL RECORDS

WE WORKED WITH:
Kanye West - Jay Z - Stevie Wonder - Michael Jackson - Germaine Jackson - Smokey Robinson - Dionne Warwick - Cheryl Lynn - The Originals -

Digital Marketing Services
SOCIAL MEDIA - STREAMING SERVICES - MUSIC DISTRIBUTION - PRESS RELEASE - PRESS DISTRIBUTION - PR

Radio Airplay and TV Commercial
TERRESTRIAL AND DIGITAL RADIO CAMPAIGN AL GENRES EXCEPT HEAVY METAL -
CABLE TV AND MAJOR NETWORK COMMERCIAL

Licensing & Booking
CONCERTS, LIVE MUSIC, EVENTS, CLUB NIGHTS - RED CARPETS -
FOREIGN LICENSING AND SUBOPUBLISHING

📞 **1-818-514-0038**
(Ext. 1)
Monday - Friday / 9am to 6pm

FIND US :

www.YourMusicConsultant.com
30721 Russell Ranch Road Suite 140 Westlake Village, USA
Email : info@yourmusicconsultant.com

Are you a songwriter or composer struggling to protect your work and releases?
Well Bernie Capodici has done all the work for you in his new book
"Modern Recording Artist Handbook, How To Guide Simplified"

Only $12.95

MUST READ FOR INDEPENDENT ARTISTS

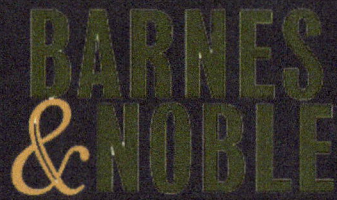

KINDLE $9.99 - HARDCOVER $22.95 - PAPERBACK $12.95

L.A. UNLIMITED

APPAREL REPRESENTATION
WITHOUT LIMITS...

- Corporate Brand Representation
- Brand Identity & Management
- Brand Consulting
- Trade Show Preparation & Participation
- Trunk Shows
- Private Label Sales
- Production Sourcing

L.A. Unlimited & Associates
30765 Pacific Coast Hwy STE 443Malibu, CA 90265

310.882.6432
sales@launlimitedinc.com

FASHION
70'S FASHION IS BACK!

HIPPIE STYLE

Hippies first came about during the peace movement of the 1960s, but it was in the '70s that the style's popularity peaked. Designers of the time picked up on the clothing items popular with those in the subculture, like fringe, oversized silhouettes, and folky details, and created something completely new. The resulting styles were worn by everyone across age and gender—they became a symbol of idealism.

ECLECTIC

While the youth of every era have their own form of rebellion, those that came of age during the '70s made it a mission to upend the strict rules of decorum their parents grew up with. Young people of the time mixed clothing of all different styles, from army surplus store finds to precious handmade knitwear.

GENDER NEUTRALDENIM EVERYTHING

Unisex clothing began gaining traction in the 1970s, the most popular items being suits, trousers, jeans, and overalls.

DENIM EVERYTHING

While denim has existed since the 19th century, it wasn't until the 1970s that the fabric became a daily fashion staple. Once youth subcultures and Hollywood got the trend going, there was no going back, and now denim is ubiquitous worldwide from the runways to the streets.

DISCO

You can't speak about the 1970s without mentioning disco. Leather, lurex, metallics, and glitter were en vogue, and this season designers took note, channeling the decade's carefree spirit into collections with a similar mentality. After a year in lockdown, imagining a wardrobe for freer times is just the dose of optimism we need.

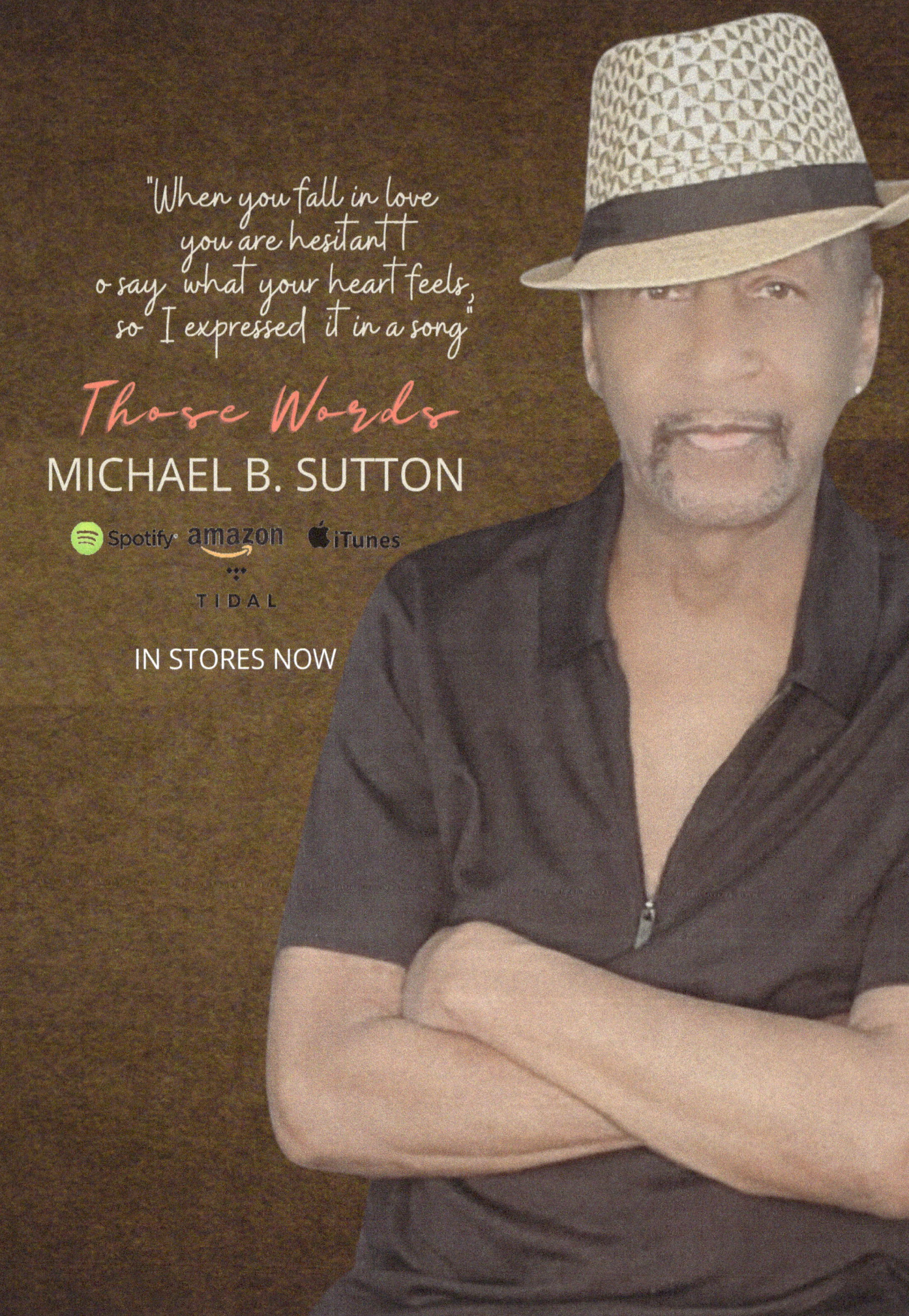

REVIVING THE ICONIC SOUND OF 90'S R&B

"THROWBACK, THE COVERS" VOL.1
A COMPILATION OF THE MOST TIMELESS 90'S R&B TRACKS

www.SaintJaimz.com

1. TOMATOES

An important component in tomatoes is lycopene, which is a powerful antioxidant that can work wonders to bring back life to your skin. The most efficient way to get healthy skin nutrient is tomato paste made from organic tomatoes. All you need to do is slice the tomatoes and make a paste, or just apply the slices on your face and then wash it with cold water.

2. JOJOBA OIL

Jojoba oil helps retain moisture in the skin thereby keeping the skin hydrated and looking fresh. It acts as a moisturiser, without clogging the pores, allowing for a healthy skin type. In addition, it also prevents the buildup of bacteria in the pores of the face, which tend to cause blackheads and acne," says Shiv Singh Mann, Founder, Desert Splendour.

3. SUGAR AND LEMON SCRUB

Looking for a natural scrub to get rid of dirt from your skin? Try sugar! Sugar is a commendable source of glycolic acid, which penetrates the skin cells and leaves you looking fresh and rejuvenated. It is a great exfoliator and prevents dryness. Make a scrub using 2 tablespoons of sugar and juice of 4 limes and massage it into your skin until the sugar dissolves. Wash your face with cold water and wipe clean.

4. RIPE BANANA

Often referred to as the common man's moisturiser and nourisher, banana works like magic in treating dry skin. All you need to do is mash a ripe banana and massage it onto the skin for 5 minutes before washing off with cold water. Even the driest of skins will thank you for it.

5. PAPAYA

This nutrition-packed fruit is a great skin cleanser. Beauty experts often suggest using slices of papaya as a natural skin cleanser because the active enzymes work wonders to remo impurities.

7. AVOCADO AND RICE POWDER MASK:

This is not only a mask but this is also an exfoliator. This is very good for people having dry and sagging surface. People who has dryness and needs Moisturization they can benefit with this. The powder will help to exfoliate and the avocado contains excellent moisturising properties. These can be very helpful.

People can mix about 1 cup of pulp of avocado which should be ripe and to this about half a teaspoon of grained rice powder.
This should be applied normally and then after 20 minutes, this should be washed off by scrubbing in gentle motions.
The mask will soften the surface and then it can be scrubbed easily.
This should be done as per requirement which can be twice a week.

8. LEMON JUICE AND OLIVE OIL MASSAGE FOR FAIRNESS SKIN:

This is very good for those having sagging and old surface. This can be good for those who have clogged pores because warm olive oil will help to open the ores. At the same time, the lemon juice helps to mildly bleach the surface and give a glowing effect.
About 1 teaspoon of good brand olive oil can be taken and slightly warmed up.
To this about 1 teaspoon of fresh lemon juice can be mixed.
Massage on for about 6 minutes and then wash off with a cleanser.
This should only be done a few times a week.
This should be avoided or the lemon juice used in less quantity if these is irritating to the person using this.

9. BESAN OR GRAM FLOUR

"Besan is an extremely neutral ingredient that is great for cleansing skin," says Dr. Indu Ballani, Delhi-based Dermatologist. It can be used for all sorts of skin to reduce dryness, acnes, sun tan, dead skin, wrinkles, blemishes, oil and dirt.

10. ALOE VERA

Saving the best for the last, there's nothing quite like aloe vera when it comes to taking care of your skin. This magical plant is loaded with compounds that can bring back life to undernourished skin. Scrape out the gel from the leaf, mash it and massage onto the skin. Let it sit there for 10 minutes and wash the skin with cold water and pat dry.

11. DAHI OR YOGHURT

"Yogurt is excellent when you have oily to combination skin. Just 2 teaspoon can be massaged daily at the end of the day and washed off. This will clean as well as prevent your skin from damage," says renowned beauty expert, Suparna Trikha.

OPENING HOURS
By Appointment Only

Call: 702-530-2615

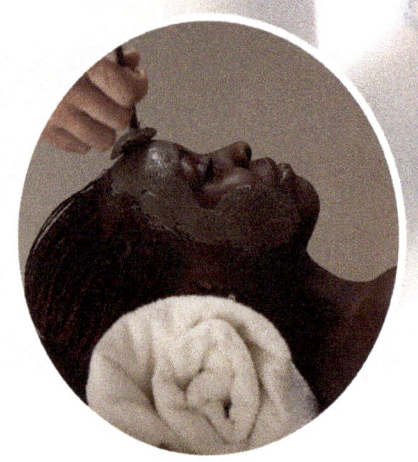

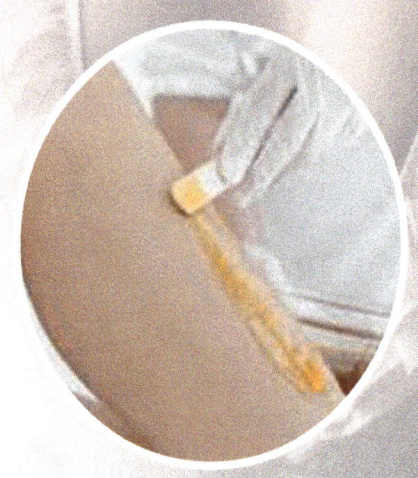

Facial Treatment
Acne - Anti-Ageing - Back Facial - Hollywood Facial

Waxing
Honey Wax - Stripeless Hard Wax Gourmet Wax

Lashes & Brows
Lash Tinting
EyeBrow Tinting

More Services

* Microdermabrasion - Dermaplaning
* Chemical Peel - Botox
* Non-invasive Lipo - Non-invasive BBL
* Body Scrub - Body Wrap - Sauna Detox
* Teeth Whitening
  Take-Home Teeth Whitening Kit

Skin & Body Treatment

Enter a world of luxury with the sisters who mastered the world of beauty. Through our carefully crafted services, your mind, body, and soul will obtain results beyond your wildest expectations. We have combined the best artists of beauty in their field with an atmosphere meant to relax and achieve any desired result.

WWW.BELLASORELLABI.COM

2801 South Valley view Blvd. Suite 4, Las Vegas, NV.89102, Tel: 702-530-2615

Best Rollerskating Movies of All Time!

Below you will find my list of the best roller skating movies. Since their invention in the 18th century, roller skates have been a turning point in human recreational history. They're fun, sporty and catchy.

Roller skates have been used as an essential US troops equipment to move infantry in World War II, as well as being a hobby, a sport and dancing equipment for boys and girls of all ages.

However, roller skates had their share of "Roller Skate Craze" moments across history, most notably in the 60s, the disco style skating 70s to 80s, the early 1990s and even today.

A lot of the roller skating obsessions have also been played out in all different kinds of roller skating and rollerblading movies. With every hit roller skating movie that included any form of roller blades or skates, the media and public went crazy over them.

Since roller skating movies have a huge impact on the roller skating culture, we're going to give you the ultimate guide to the best roller skating movies ever made.

1. ROLLER BOOGIE

Roller Boogie was released in December 1979. The movie features Linda Blair as Terry Barkley and the famous Competitive Artistic Roller Skater Jim Bray as Bobby James. Although it was planned for Jim Bray to play Bobby James only as a stunt double, after the producers' failure to find an actor they liked, they decided to cast Jim Bray instead. With Jim's several skating awards and amazing stunt moves, the producers decided to hire him as Bobby.

The movie plot is about Terry, a neglected teenage girl with wealthy parents who wanted her to make it into the Juilliard School for Art and Music as a flutist. However, her parents had no idea how much their daughter hated playing the flute.

While accompanying her friend Lana, who was skating on the Broadwalk of Venice Beach, California, Terry encounters Booby James for the first time, a talented roller skater who believes that he can make it into the next Olympics.

MOVIES

2. XANADU

Xanadu is a fantasy roller-skating musical film released in 1980. Starring the beautiful Olivia Newton-John, Gene Kelly, and Micheal Beck, Xanadu is packed with a group of talented dancers, actors, and musicians.

The movie presents an excellent model of what the late 70s musicals and the disco style's golden era. The movie is about a painter (Michael Beck) who is fascinated by a woman he finds on the background of one of his photograph assignments.

He then begins his quest to find her in the auditorium, where the photo was taken. He then finds out that Kira (Olivia Newton-John) is in fact a Greek muse whose job it is to help people follow their dreams.

She then leads him to team up with an old friend (Gene Kelly) to pursue their fantasy of having a roller-skating disco.

Although the plot is the weakest point of the movie, it still features some astounding music, excellent cinematography, and well-prepared choreography.

If you enjoy musicals, with a sweet tinge of fantasy and retro style 70s disco themes, then you're in for a treat!

3. SKATETOWN, U.S.A

The movie was produced in late 1979 to hop on the roller skating bandwagon. Skatetown, U.S.A is another movie that capitalized on the short-lived era of roller disco craze that hit the United States back in the 1970s.

Similar to most roller skating movies at that time, the movie didn't feature a strong plot. However, the movie features a wide range of television stars such as Scott Baio, Maureen McCormick, Flip Wilson, and the debut of one of Hollywood's Hotshots, Patrick Swayze.

Skatetown, U.S.A's plot is simply about a fierce rivalry between a street gang leader Stan Nelson, who was played by Greg Bradford, and a local young roller skater named Ace Johnson, played by Patrick Swayze, for a prize of $1,000 and a moped.

The movie highlights some of Swayze's iconic moves and skating stunts. It also had almost non-stop diegetic background music playing along with the whole movie.

TOP TIPS

CREATIVE WAYS TO SELL MORE MERCH

MAKE YOUR ONLINE STORE EASY TO FIND & INTEGRATE YOUR PRODUCTS INTO YOUR CONTENT

You don't want fans to have to go searching for your merch booth in a dark venue, right? The same principle holds true for online sales. Make your store easy to find on your website. There should be a link in the top navigation. You may even want to call attention to featured items right on your home page.

The content you create is another natural place to plug your merch. Whether that means wearing your merch in your videos, promoting it directly in social media posts, or building it into the creative concept of your next piece of content (such as a contest prize).

Here are some of the channels you can explore and approaches you can take:

Instagram: Tag your merch in your posts and stories and curate your own Instagram Shop on your profile.

YouTube: Share links to your products in your video description or cards, with a call-to-action at the end of your video itself.

TikTok: Partner with other TikTok creators to get them to create content with your merch.

Buy button: If you have a separate website or blog outside of your merch store, you can embed your products or collections there as well.

The best way to go about connecting your merch to your content is up to you—you know your audience best, after all. For Seek Discomfort, that meant hosting a fashion show in their backyard.

REMARKETING TO YOUR EXISTING AUDIENCE

What about spending money to promote your merch through ads? In other contexts, you may want to run prospecting ads—fishing for new audiences to purchase your products—but with merch, retargeting is your friend.

Retargeting lets you promote ads to your existing audience based on specific criteria, such as whether they follow you on Instagram or have already made a purchase. Many ad platforms (Google, Facebook, YouTube, TikTok, Snapchat) allow you to run retargeting ads, as long as you have their advertising pixel installed on your website or customer emails you can upload to build an audience of fans to retarget.

"That's where you're going to have really high engagement and ROI," says Zack. "Whereas with prospecting, most of the time people aren't going to buy merchandise from someone they've never heard of before. So that's where the bulk of your energy from paid media spend should go."

Needless to say, if you've been building your email list, that's definitely a channel you'll want to use to promote your merch.

TOP TIPS

TOGETHER WE CAN END HUNGER WORLD FOOD PROGRAM USA

The global food supply consistently produces enough food to feed every single person in the world. And yet, nearly 1 billion people are undernourished and another 1 billion are going hungry every year.

Last month, world leaders met at the United Nations to define the sustainable development agenda through 2030. This is important, because there is tremendous power in coming together across 193 countries to discuss what it takes to build a world we can all live and thrive in.

Today on World Food Day, Sustainable Development Goal #2—End hunger, achieve food security and improved nutrition and promote sustainable agriculture—is especially meaningful.

Ending hunger means changing the way we think and act about the world and sustainability. As President of Food Care at Sealed Air, the reality of hunger and the need for a sustainable food chain is always on my mind.

We work every day to create smarter packaging, improve our food safety and hygiene practices and provide our customers with innovative packaging that extends the shelf life of food.

We know that food waste is more than a business issue. It's also a health and food security issue. Each year, 1.3 billion tons of food end up rotting in retail and consumer bins, or spoiling due to poor transportation and harvesting practices. Food waste reduction and food safety are vital to creating a sustainable future.

To solve some of these issues with true solutions and not temporary band aids, we must rely on purposeful innovation and community involvement.
From food packaging and storage to supply chain to education, there is tremendous power in what we can achieve and how we can help, when we come together and think outside of the box.

At Sealed Air, we are doing this today in the communities we serve through programs like Fresher for Longer and our partnerships in China with the World Wildlife Fund and the China Chain Store and Franchise Association to improve the safety of the poultry supply chain and reduce food waste.

We can't succeed in ending world hunger if we try to act alone. Making a difference requires a mindset that is capable of seeing value beyond economic impact, and publicizing the issue. Cooperation and innovation are what it will take to preserve our resources and build a sustainable future.

HELP STOP HUNGER & POVERTY

There are 1 billion impoverished kids around the world

JOIN OUR CAMPAIGN TO HELP GIVE THEM BETTER LIVES.

WFP
World Food Program USA
wfpusa.org